PEARL HARBOR

A DAY OF INFAMY

By Steve White Illustrated by Jerrold Spahn

rosen publishing's
**rosen
central**

New York

Published in 2007 by The Rosen Publishing Group, Inc.
29 East 21st Street, New York, NY 10010

First edition, 2007

Photo Credits: pp. 4 and 5 (Kimmel) Malcolm MacGregor © Osprey Publishing Ltd. (Yamamoto and Pearl Harbor) National Archives and Records Administration; pp. 6 and 7 (Nagumo and Shaw) National Archives and Records Administration; pp. 44 and 45 (Hitler) Courtesy of Imperial War Museum, (wreckage and planes) National Archives and Records Administration

Karl Bollers, Editor, Rosen Book Works
Simone Drinkwater, Series Editor, Osprey Publishing
Nel Yomtov, Series Editor, Rosen Book Works

Library of Congress Cataloging-in-Publication Data

White Steve D. (Steve David), 1964–
    Pearl Harbor: a day of infamy / by Steve White.— 1st ed.
    p. cm. — (Graphic battles of World War II)
    Includes bibliographical references and index.
    ISBN-13   978-1-4042-0785-1 (lib.)   978-1-4042-7428-0 (pbk.)
    ISBN-10   1-4042-0785-6 (lib.)   1-4042-7428-6 (pbk.)
    6-pack ISBN-13   978-1-4042-7429-7   6-pack ISBN-10   1-4042-7429-4

    1. Pearl Harbor (Hawaii), Attack on, 1941–Juvenile literature.
    I. Title. II. Series.

    D767.92.W48 2007
    940.54'26693–dc22

                                        2006007515

CONTENTS

WORLD WAR II, 1939–1945

Even after the end of World War I (1914–1918), the world was still a hostile place. To avoid more fighting, the United States worked to build good relations with other countries and to basically mind its own business.

However, Japan was becoming aggressive toward its neighbors, especially China. Italy invaded Ethiopia in 1936. Germany, under Adolf Hitler, took Austria and Czechoslovakia in 1938. In 1939, Germany invaded Poland. France and England then declared war on Germany. Still, the United States did not get involved in the growing worldwide tensions.

On December 7, 1941, Japanese forces attacked the U.S. naval base at Pearl Harbor, Hawaii. The next day, America declared war on Japan. Germany then declared war on America. The greatest conflict in the history of mankind had begun.

KEY COMMANDERS

Admiral Husband E. Kimmel
Commander of the Pacific Fleet at the time of the Pearl Harbor attack. He was blamed for America's unreadiness for the attack and was relieved of his command days later.

President Franklin Delano Roosevelt
President of the United States at the time of the Pearl Harbor attack. Roosevelt died before the Japanese surrender in August 1945.

Admiral Isoroku Yamamoto
Commander of the Imperial Japanese Navy and a strong believer in the superiority of air power in battle. He planned the attack on Pearl Harbor.

Commander Mitsuo Fuchida
A Japanese navy pilot, he led the first wave of attacks on Pearl Harbor. He was badly injured at the Battle of Midway.

In its efforts to move into the modern age, Japan realized it had little or no oil, gas, or other raw materials. Japanese military commanders decided to expand into countries that had these materials. In 1931, Japan invaded China, beginning a long and bloody war. Japanese commander Admiral Isoroku Yamamoto realized that the key to waging war and expanding Japan's empire was air power. In 1936, he began organizing a naval air arm, using aircraft carriers.

Japan's increasing hostility concerned the United States and Europe. When war exploded in Europe in 1939, Japan knew that the Europeans would not want to extend that war into Asia. They saw this war as an opportunity to invade other nations. However, not all Japanese thought expansion was a good idea. Some officials feared war with the United

(background) The Hawaiian island of Oahu was home to the U.S. naval bases Pearl Harbor and Kaneohe and to the airfields Haleiwa, Ewa, Wheeler, Hickam, and Bellows Field. (right) Admiral Husband E. Kimmel was the U. S. Navy's senior admiral in 1941 and was the naval commander in charge of Pearl Harbor at the time of the attack.

States. These people were looking for a peaceful settlement to the two nations' differences. However, "hawks"–those in power who favored war–set a time limit on such a solution.

In spring 1940, the U.S. Pacific Fleet moved to Pearl Harbor on Oahu, Hawaii. The Japanese believed that the United States could use the islands as a base to strike them. They saw the move to Pearl Harbor as a threat to Japanese security. Relations between the two countries worsened. President Franklin D. Roosevelt then signed a secret order that allowed former members of the U.S. military to fight against the Japanese in China. He also banned the export of scrap metal, steel, and aviation fuel to Japan.

The Japanese now had three choices: give in to American demands and leave China, wait for their fuel to run out, or attack and seize resource-rich areas. Admiral Yamamoto thought that his best option was to strike first. He knew that Japan could not defeat America in a long war. He decided on a quick, surprise attack to crush the U.S. Navy.

In early 1941, Yamamoto began planning for the conquest of those areas of Asia that Japan desired. Part of that plan was to attack and cripple the U.S. Navy at Pearl Harbor. The Japanese gave themselves a time limit. If peaceful efforts to solve its differences with America had not succeeded by November 23, 1941, Japan would attack.

Japanese spies began reporting on American ships and aircraft in and

Japanese Admiral Isoroku Yamamoto did not want to go to war with the United States. However, when Japan decided to do so, he knew his nation must succeed. The plan to attack Pearl Harbor was his.

around Pearl Harbor. Of particular interest were U.S. aircraft carriers, which the Japanese feared above all other American vessels. The Americans worried about sabotage or an invasion from the sea. They did not expect an air attack because they thought the harbor was too shallow for torpedoes to be dropped successfully.

As Japan prepared to attack, U.S. intelligence services broke some of the codes used by the Japanese in their messages. American commanders learned that some kind of attack would come at the end of November. However, the decoded material was often incomplete and did not reach the right people. Also, nothing in the reports indicated Pearl Harbor was the target, so life around the base carried on as normal.

Peace talks in Washington, D.C., continued between American and Japanese diplomats. After many failed attempts, the Japanese ambassador to America, Admiral Kichisaburo Nomura, was ordered to end his efforts to find a peaceful solution by November 29. The deadline was final.

On November 26, a fleet of Japanese warships set sail toward Pearl Harbor. It included six aircraft carriers, carrying 441 aircraft. They were escorted by two battleships, two

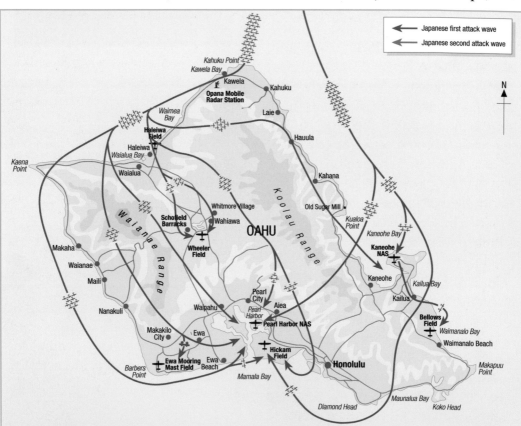

On December 7, 1941, hundreds of Japanese planes took off from aircraft carriers to attack U.S. military bases on the Hawaiian island of Oahu. The attack came in two waves in which American naval bases and airfields were bombed and torpedoed. The following day, the United States declared war on Japan, officially beginning America's involvement in World War II.

(left) Vice Admiral Chuichi Nagumo was an expert in torpedo warfare. He commanded the Japanese 1st Air Fleet that attacked Pearl Harbor. (right) The area where U.S. ships were anchored in Pearl Harbor was called Battleship Row. The ships were easy targets for the attacking Japanese planes. One of the worst hit was USS *Shaw*, which exploded into flames.

heavy cruisers, six destroyers, and several submarines. Five midget submarines were also due to launch from larger subs. These were to enter the harbor and torpedo American ships.

On November 27, U.S. leaders in Washington warned commanders in Hawaii to be extra alert. However, the islands had no defenses prepared.

On December 2, Yamamoto told Chuichi Nagumo, commander of the Japanese Fleet, to open his orders. They read, "Our Empire has decided to go to war against the United States, Britain, and Holland in early December." The date was set at December 7, Hawaiian time.

One concern of the Japanese was reports that none of the feared American aircraft carriers were in Pearl Harbor. Even so, the attack would proceed.

On December 7, Ambassador Nomura was told to expect a message

from the Japanese embassy that was to be delivered to U.S. Secretary of State Cordell Hull by 1:00 P.M., Washington time. In this message, Japan would declare an end to peaceful negotiations with the United States. However, even if the message had been delivered on time, the United States would have had little time to react before the attack began.

Due to delays in decoding the message, it was *not* delivered on time. Nomura finally delivered it at 2:20 P.M., long after the attack on Pearl Harbor had begun. He had not been told of the air strike and, although he knew the message was important, Nomura had no idea just how important it was.

PEARL HARBOR
A DAY OF INFAMY

SUNDAY, DECEMBER 7, 1941. THE FINAL COUNTDOWN TO THE UNITED STATES' ENTRY INTO WORLD WAR II BEGINS.

3:42 A.M. THE DECK OFFICER ABOARD AMERICAN MINESWEEPER *CONDOR* SPOTS SOMETHING. THE SHIP IS JUST TWO MILES FROM THE ENTRANCE TO PEARL HARBOR, ON OAHU, HAWAII.

IT LOOKS LIKE A PERISCOPE.

THE *CONDOR* FLASHES A MESSAGE TO U.S. DESTROYER *WARD*:

"SIGHTED SUBMERGED SUBMARINE ON WESTERLY COURSE, SPEED NINE KNOTS." *WARD* INVESTIGATES BUT FINDS NOTHING.

6:00 A.M. U.S.S. *ENTERPRISE* LAUNCHES 18 *SBD* SCOUT AIRCRAFT. THEIR DESTINATION IS FORD ISLAND, PEARL HARBOR.

THEIR EXPECTED TIME OF ARRIVAL IS 8:00 A.M.

6:10 A.M., DAWN. THE SUN RISES ON A FLEET OF IMPERIAL JAPANESE NAVY WARSHIPS 250 MILES NORTH OF OAHU.

CENTERPIECE OF THE FLEET ARE SIX AIRCRAFT CARRIERS UNDER THE COMMAND OF VICE ADMIRAL CHUICHI NAGUMO: *AKAGI, HIRYU, KAGA, SHOKAKU, SORYU,* AND *ZUIKAKU.*

NAGUMO ORDERS THAT THE JAPANESE FLEET SHOULD "LAUNCH A RESOLUTE SURPRISE ATTACK ON AND DEAL A FATAL BLOW TO THE ENEMY."

THAT TIME HAS NOW COME.

6:15 A.M. NAGUMO, ABOARD HIS FLAGSHIP, *AKAGI,* GIVES THE ORDER TO LAUNCH THE FIRST WAVE TO ATTACK PEARL HARBOR.

THE CARRIERS TURN NORTHEAST AND BEGIN LAUNCHING AIRCRAFT. FIRST AWAY ARE THE *A6M2* MODEL 21 "ZEKES" FIGHTERS. THEY ARE KNOWN AS "ZEROES" BY THE ALLIES BECAUSE THEY DIDN'T KNOW THE JAPANESE NAMES.

9

AS THE ZEROES CIRCLE OVERHEAD, THE TORPEDO AND DIVE-BOMBERS LIFT OFF AND CLIMB TO JOIN THEM.

THE DIVE-BOMBERS ARE *AICHI D3A1 MODEL 11S*, KNOWN AS *"VALS"* BY THE ALLIES. THEY CAN CARRY AN 816-POUND BOMB LOAD MORE THAN 900 MILES.

IN THE COMING ATTACK, TORPEDOES WILL BE DROPPED IN THE SEA BY *NAKAJIMA B5N2 TYPE 97S*, KNOWN AS *"KATES"* BY THE ALLIES.

THE 183 AIRCRAFT OF THE FIRST ATTACK WAVE FORM HUGE V-SHAPED FORMATIONS. THEN THEY TURN SOUTH BY SOUTHWEST TOWARD THEIR TARGET.

IT'S A BEAUTIFUL MORNING.

6:30 A.M. THE U.S. SUPPLY SHIP **ANTARES** SPOTS WHAT IT THINKS IS A SUBMARINE. IT INFORMS THE U.S.S. **WARD**.

A **CATALINA PBY** SCOUT ALSO SPOTS THE SUB. IT IS A JAPANESE **KO-HYOTEKI MIDGET SUBMARINE**. THE CATALINA DROPS A SMOKE MARKER ON IT.

THE SUB IS ONE OF FIVE DUE TO ATTACK PEARL HARBOR.

6:45 A.M. LIEUTENANT WILLIAM W. OUTERBRIDGE, WHO HAS BEEN IN COMMAND OF **WARD** FOR ONLY TWO DAYS, ORDERS THE SHIP TO OPEN FIRE.

ONE ROUND HITS THE SUB'S CONNING TOWER, AND IT SUBMERGES. THESE ARE THE FIRST SHOTS OF THE BATTLE.

THE **WARD** AND THE PBY DROP DEPTH CHARGES ALONG THE ASSUMED COURSE OF THE SUB.

THE SUB DOES NOT REAPPEAR.

OUTERBRIDGE SENDS A CODED MESSAGE TO HIS HEADQUARTERS.

ATTACKED, FIRED UPON, AND DROPPED DEPTH CHARGES!

THE MESSAGE IS DELAYED IN DECODING.

7:00 A.M. COMMANDER MITSUO FUCHIDA LEADS THE FIRST WAVE OF JAPANESE AIRCRAFT.

HE KNOWS THAT HAWAIIAN RADIO STATIONS OFTEN PLAY MUSIC ALL NIGHT LONG WHEN AMERICAN AIRCRAFT ARE EXPECTED FROM THE UNITED STATES MAINLAND.

THIS IS ONE SUCH NIGHT.

HE PICKS UP THE RADIO STATION LOUD AND CLEAR AND ORDERS HIS CREWS TO USE THE SIGNAL AS A DIRECTIONAL LOCATOR.

7:02 A.M. ON OPANA RIDGE, OAHU, AMERICAN PRIVATES JOSEPH LOCKARD AND GEORGE ELLIOTT MAN AN *SCR-270 MOBILE RADAR STATION.*

THERE IS A BLIP ON THE RADAR. A **BIG** BLIP.

IS THIS THING BROKEN? THERE MUST BE 50 PLANES ON THE SCREEN!

CALL FORT SHAFTER – QUICK!

AT 7:06 A.M., THE PRIVATES CALL FORT SHAFTER INFORMATION CENTER, HUB OF THE RADAR CHAIN.

ELLIOTT IS TOLD THAT ALL SIGNAL CORPS PERSONNEL ARE AT BREAKFAST.

THE BLIP IS NOW ONLY 100 MILES NORTH, CLOSING IN ON PEARL HARBOR.

7:15 A.M. 260 MILES NORTH OF OAHU, 168 AIRCRAFT OF THE SECOND WAVE LAUNCH AND TURN TOWARD HAWAII.

7:20 A.M. IN THE RADAR STATION ON OPANA RIDGE, LOCKARD AND ELLIOTT GET A CALL FROM FORT SHAFTER.

YOU'RE PROBABLY LOOKING AT THE B-17S COMING FROM THE MAINLAND. DON'T WORRY ABOUT IT.

7:33 A.M. IN WASHINGTON, D.C., U.S. CODEBREAKERS CRACK THE LAST SECTION OF A 14-PART JAPANESE MESSAGE DUE TO BE DELIVERED TO U.S. OFFICIALS AT 1:00 P.M. THE LANGUAGE IS AGGRESSIVE AND THREATENING. IT SOUNDS LIKE WAR.

ARMY CHIEF OF STAFF GENERAL GEORGE C. MARSHALL SENDS A WARNING TO HAWAIIAN ARMY HEADQUARTERS.

WEATHER CONDITIONS BLACK OUT RADIO COMMUNICATIONS WITH HAWAII SO THE MESSAGE IS TELEGRAMMED.

IT REMAINS UNREAD UNTIL 3:00 P.M. -- FAR TOO LATE.

7:38 A.M. AN *AICHI E13A1 TYPE O "JAKE"* FLOATPLANE FROM THE CRUISER *CHIKUMA* ARRIVES OVER PEARL HARBOR AND REPORTS ON THE U.S. FLEET. THE JAKE ALSO REPORTS THAT THERE ARE NO U.S. SHIPS AT THE DEEPER PORT ON THE NEARBY ISLAND OF MAUI.

ENEMY AT ANCHOR. NINE BATTLESHIPS, ONE HEAVY CRUISER, SIX LIGHT CRUISERS.

BECAUSE THE PORT AT PEARL HARBOR WAS SHALLOW, THE JAPANESE HAD MODIFIED THEIR MARK 91 TORPEDOES.

THE AMERICANS BELIEVE PEARL HARBOR IS TOO SHALLOW FOR CONVENTIONAL TORPEDOES TO WORK.

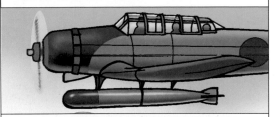

HOWEVER, THE JAPANESE HAVE ADDED WOODEN FINS TO THEIR TORPEDOES FOR EXTRA STABILITY AND BUOYANCY. SHALLOW WATER IS NOT A PROBLEM.

7:40 A.M. AS THE JAPANESE VANISH OFF THE RADAR AT OPANA RIDGE, COMMANDER FUCHIDA'S KATE DROPS BENEATH THE CLOUDS.

THE SKY IS EMPTY OF U.S. FIGHTERS. OAHU LIES AHEAD.

7:49 A.M. FUCHIDA ORDERS HIS AIRCRAFT INTO ATTACK FORMATION BY FIRING A FLARE ...

BUT THERE IS CONFUSION. THE PILOTS THINK THAT THEY HAVE BEEN ORDERED TO ATTACK AND TURN INLAND.

HIS AIRCRAFT BEGIN THEIR ATTACK RUNS ON EWA FIELD AND KANEOHE NAVAL AIR STATION (NAS).

7:51 A.M. KANEOHE NAS, HOME TO THE PBY CATALINAS OF NAVAL PATROL WING 1, IS STRAFED BY ZEROES FOR TEN MINUTES AND SHATTERED TO PIECES.

7:53 A.M. SIX MORE ZEROES ATTACK EWA MARINE AIR CORPS STATION, BLASTING AIRCRAFT ON THE RUNWAY.

7:55 A.M. VAL DIVE-BOMBERS RAIN THEIR LOADS DOWN UPON HICKAM FIELD ARMY AIR BASE.

AAARGH!

A BOMB HITS A **B-18 BOLO**, KILLING 22 MEN. HANGARS BURST INTO FLAMES.

IT'S TOO NICE OUT TO SLEEP. WHY DON'T WE HEAD OVER TO HALEIWA FOR A SWIM?

AT WHEELER FIELD, EIGHT MILES NORTHWEST OF PEARL HARBOR, SECOND LIEUTENANTS KEN TAYLOR AND GEORGE WELCH HAVE BEEN PARTYING ALL NIGHT ...

WHAT THE--?!

7:51 A.M. 25 VALS ATTACK THE 120 U.S. FIGHTERS THAT ARE LINED UP ON THE WHEELER AIRFIELD.

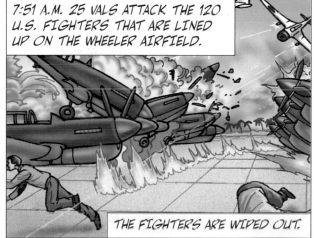

THE FIGHTERS ARE WIPED OUT.

15

WELCH CALLS HALEIWA FIELD, AN AUXILIARY AIR BASE USED BY AIRCRAFT FROM WHEELER FIELD.

GET TWO P-40S READY! THE JAPANESE ARE HERE!

AFTER A DRIVE TO HALEIWA, DURING WHICH THEY WERE STRAFED THREE TIMES, WELCH AND TAYLOR FIND THEIR P-40 TOMAHAWKS READY TO GO.

THE U.S. AIRMEN MEET 12 VALS OVER EWA FIELD.

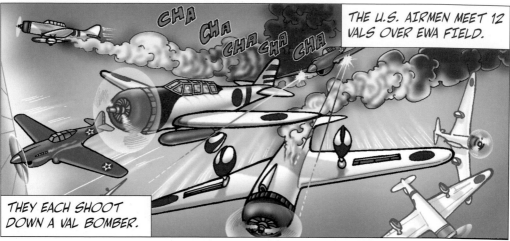

CHA CHA CHA CHA CHA

THEY EACH SHOOT DOWN A VAL BOMBER.

TAYLOR PULLS UP, AND AS HE ROLLS IN, SEES A LONE VAL HEADING OUT TO SEA.

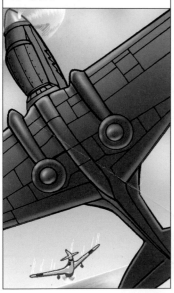

TAYLOR GIVES FULL THROTTLE TO THE FIGHTER AND GETS BEHIND THE BOMBER.

HIS MARKSMANSHIP IS EXCELLENT. THE VAL BREAKS UP UNDER A HAIL OF FIRE.

MEANWHILE, WELCH IS HIT. HE DIVES INTO CLOUD COVER.

!@#$!

THE DAMAGE TO WELCH'S P-40 IS MINOR. HE CLIMBS OUT OF THE CLOUDS, ONLY TO FIND ANOTHER VAL AHEAD OF HIM.

WITH ONLY ONE MACHINE GUN WORKING ON HIS PLANE, WELCH FLAMES THE BOMBER, AND IT CRASHES INTO THE SEA.

YES!

9:20 A.M. TAYLOR AND WELCH ARE LOW ON FUEL AND AMMUNITION. THEY LAND AT WHEELER BETWEEN JAPANESE AIR ATTACKS.

ALL THE SPARE STUFF IS IN THE HANGAR THAT'S ON FIRE!

WE'RE OUT OF AMMO!

THE BRAVE MECHANICS HEAD INTO THE BLAZING HANGAR.

AMAZINGLY, THEY MAKE IT OUT ALIVE!

KRAK
KRAK
KRAK

9:30 A.M. 16 VALS, RETURNING TO KAGA FROM PEARL HARBOR, STRAFE WHEELER FIELD AS TAYLOR AND WELCH TAKE OFF IN OPPOSITE DIRECTIONS.

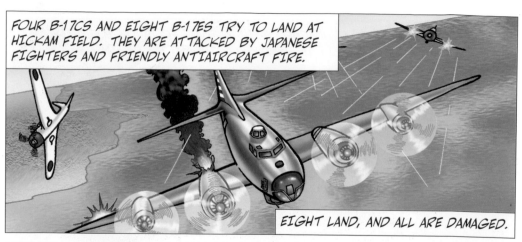

FOUR B-17CS AND EIGHT B-17ES TRY TO LAND AT HICKAM FIELD. THEY ARE ATTACKED BY JAPANESE FIGHTERS AND FRIENDLY ANTIAIRCRAFT FIRE.

EIGHT LAND, AND ALL ARE DAMAGED.

TWO HEAD FOR HALEIWA FIELD. ONE LANDS ON A CIVILIAN RUNWAY ...

... AND ONE COLLAPSES AS IT REACHES BELLOWS FIELD ON THE SOUTHEASTERN END OF THE ISLAND.

16 KATES FROM *SORYU* AND *HIRYU* HEAD TOWARD THE AMERICAN SHIPS ON THE NORTHWEST SIDE OF FORD ISLAND.

BOTH SHIPS SHUDDER UNDER THE IMPACT. *RALEIGH* BEGINS TO ROLL OVER TO ONE SIDE.

SIX BOMBERS RELEASE THEIR TORPEDOES AT *UTAH* AND *RALEIGH*.

7:56 A.M. MORE KATES ATTACK THE LIGHT CRUISER **HELENA**, WHICH HAS THE MINELAYER **OGLALA** BERTHED BESIDE IT.

WITH THE SUN IN THEIR EYES, JAPANESE PILOTS THINK THEY'RE FIRING AT A BATTLESHIP.

THEIR TORPEDOES PASS UNDER **OGLALA** AND HIT THE STARBOARD SIDE OF **HELENA**.

24 KATES FROM **AKAGI** AND **KAGA** START DOWN TOWARD BATTLESHIP ROW AND THEIR PRIZED TARGETS THAT ARE MOORED THERE.

HA-HA! WE GOT HER!

AIR RAID! AIR RAID! THIS IS A REAL ATTACK! REAL PLANES! REAL BOMBS!

7:58 A.M. TORPEDOES SLAM THE BATTLESHIPS **WEST VIRGINIA** AND **OKLAHOMA**.

ON SOME SHIPS, AN ALARM SOUNDS. ON OTHERS, THERE IS NO TIME. SAILORS SIMPLY RUN TO THEIR BATTLE STATIONS.

8:00 A.M. THE *CALIFORNIA* IS HIT BY TORPEDOES. ONE ... TWO ... THREE ...

OKLAHOMA IS HAMMERED BY BLOW AFTER BLOW. IT BEGINS TO ROLL TO ONE SIDE AND IS LISTING BADLY.

AAARRGGHH!

RESCUE PARTIES STRUGGLE WITH THE WOUNDED. THERE IS NO POWER, NO GUNS. THE AMMUNITION IS IN LOCKERS THAT NO ONE CAN OPEN.

AFTER EIGHT TORPEDO HITS, THE BATTLESHIP'S EXECUTIVE OFFICER, COMMANDER J. L. KENWORTHY, GIVES HIS MEN AN ORDER THAT NO COMMANDER EVER WANTS TO GIVE ...

ABANDON SHIP, MEN! ABANDON SHIP!

SAILORS RUSH OVER THE STARBOARD SIDE.

THEY CAN WALK DOWN THE SIDE OF THE *OKLAHOMA* INTO THE WATER BECAUSE IT IS LISTING SO BADLY.

FA-KOOM

A NINTH TORPEDO FINISHES *OKLAHOMA* AND IT SLOWLY CAPSIZES. NOTHING BUT ITS BELLY REMAINS ABOVE THE WATER.

MEN ARE TRAPPED BELOWDECK. THEY STRUGGLE TO HOLD THEIR BREATH LONG ENOUGH TO FIND A WAY OUT.

THOSE THAT DO GET OUT FIND THAT THE SURFACE OF THE WATER IS ON FIRE WITH OIL.

AAARGH!

HELP US, PLEASE!!

OKLAHOMA BEARS THE BRUNT OF THE ATTACKS. *MARYLAND*, MOORED NEXT TO IT, IS ALMOST UNTOUCHED.

MARYLAND LOSES ONLY FOUR MEN IN THE ATTACK. OKLAHOMA LOSES 415.

8:05 A.M. THE FIVE-INCH AND 50-CALIBER GUNS ABOARD *NEVADA* OPEN UP.

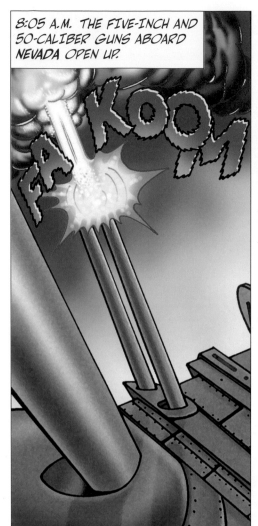

THE GUNS SET FIRE TO AN INCOMING KATE, BUT THE BURNING AIRCRAFT STILL MANAGES TO RELEASE ITS TORPEDO.

THE TORPEDO HITS *NEVADA'S* PORT BOW AND CAUSES FLOODING AND LISTING. COUNTER-FLOODING STABILIZES THE SHIP.

8:05 A.M. 49 KATES ARRIVE OVER BATTLESHIP ROW. THEY ARE OPERATING AS HIGH-ALTITUDE BOMBERS.

EACH ONE IS CARRYING AN 1,800-POUND BOMB.

THEIR TARGETS ARE THE BATTLESHIPS *ARIZONA, MARYLAND,* AND *TENNESSEE.* THE SHIPS ARE PROTECTED FROM TORPEDOES BY THE SHIPS ALONGSIDE THEM.

8:05 A.M. THE REPAIR SHIP, U.S.S. *VESTAL*, OPENS FIRE.

MOMENTS LATER, A BOMB HITS NUMBER FOUR TURRET ABOARD *ARIZONA*.

ANOTHER BOMB STRIKES THE FRONT OF THE SHIP.

8:06 A.M. ANOTHER BOMB PENETRATES ONE OF *ARIZONA'S* AMMUNITION STORAGES. ALL OF THE SHIP'S AMMUNITION IS SET ON FIRE.

A MASSIVE FIREBALL ERUPTS LIKE A VOLCANO FROM THE SHIP. 1,200 MEN ARE KILLED, AND THE VESSEL IS NEARLY DESTROYED.

THE POWER OF THE BLAST FROM **ARIZONA** BLOWS MEN ON **VESTAL** OVER THE SIDE.

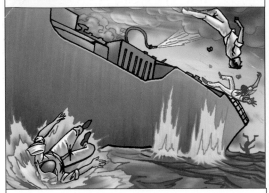

AMAZINGLY, IT ALSO BLOWS OUT THE FIRES ABOARD **VESTAL**. SURPRISINGLY LITTLE DAMAGE IS DONE TO THE SHIP.

VESTAL COMMANDER CASSIN YOUNG IS ONE OF THOSE BLOWN INTO THE WATER.

NOOO!

HELP!

YOUNG SWIMS BACK TO THE **VESTAL**. HE RALLIES THE MEN WHO ARE PREPARING TO LEAVE THE SHIP.

STAY WHERE YOU ARE! NO ONE IS ABANDONING SHIP UNTIL THE ORDER IS GIVEN!

YOUNG MAKES HIS WAY TO THE ENGINE ROOM. HE HELPS TRY TO STOP THE SHIP FROM FLOODING.

COME ON! USE THESE WOODEN BEAMS TO STOP THE WATER!

YOUNG THEN HEADS FOR THE BRIDGE. HE ORDERS THE **VESTAL** TO MOVE AWAY FROM THE EXPLODING **ARIZONA**.

THE SHIP'S STEERING GEAR IS DAMAGED AND THE ENGINES ARE STRUGGLING. A TUG HELPS PULL IT CLEAR.

9:45 A.M. ONCE MOVING, **VESTAL** STARTS TO LIST AND SINK. YOUNG ORDERS THE TUG TO BEACH HER.

FORD ISLAND. THE FIRES THREATEN TO EXPLODE THE HUGE FUEL STORAGE TANKS. SOME SAILORS RUN TO GET FIRE HOSES, BUT **ARIZONA** HAS COLLAPSED AND CUT OFF THE WATER SUPPLY.

WHAT'S WRONG WITH THESE?!

WHY WON'T THEY WORK?

WITH THE HOSES USELESS, THE SPRINKLER SYSTEM IS TURNED ON TO KEEP THE TANKS COOL.

THE TANKER **NEOSHO** IS MOORED NEXT TO THE FUEL TANKS ON SHORE.

NEOSHO EMPTIES ITS FUEL TANKS TO PREVENT AN EXPLOSION. HOWEVER, MEN ON BOARD ARE STILL WORRIED IT COULD TRIGGER TERRIBLE FIRES IF HIT.

388

ANOTHER VESSEL MAKING FOR SAFER WATERS IS THE DESTROYER **HELM.**

HELM JOINS THE GUNS THAT ARE FIRING FROM SHORE AND SHOOTS DOWN A ZERO.

KABOOM

WA CHOOM

8:10 A.M. BACK AT BATTLESHIP ROW, BOMBS HAVE STRUCK **WEST VIRGINIA**, WHICH IS NOW SINKING FAST.

WEST VIRGINIA'S MESS ATTENDANT, DORIS "DORIE" MILLER, THE FLEET BOXING CHAMPION, CARRIES WOUNDED SAILORS TO SAFE GROUND.

MILLER IS THEN ORDERED TO THE BRIDGE TO HELP THE SHIP'S CAPTAIN, MERVYN S. BENNION. THE CAPTAIN HAS BEEN SERIOUSLY WOUNDED BY SHRAPNEL.

UNABLE TO HELP HIS CAPTAIN ANY FURTHER, MILLER MANS AN ANTIAIRCRAFT GUN AND FIRES UNTIL HE RUNS OUT OF AMMUNITION.

HE MANAGES TO HIT A VAL THAT FLASHES PAST HIM.

COME ON! COME ON!

MEN DESPERATELY TRY TO PUT OUT THE FIRES ABOARD WEST VIRGINIA. THEY PUSH THE DEBRIS OVER THE SIDE.

HAVING ALSO BEEN HIT BY A JAPANESE TORPEDO, THE WEST VIRGINIA SLOWLY SINKS.

WEST VIRGINIA WEDGES THE TENNESSEE AGAINST THE HARBOR RAILINGS.

105 OF WEST VIRGINIA'S CREW ARE DEAD. TENNESSEE LOSES ONLY FIVE MEN.

8:12 A.M. MEANWHILE, ADMIRAL HUSBAND E. KIMMEL DICTATES A MESSAGE TO WARN WASHINGTON AND THE PACIFIC FLEET.

HOSTILITIES WITH JAPAN COMMENCED WITH AIR RAID ON PEARL HARBOR.

8:17 A.M. *HELM* LEAVES PEARL HARBOR FOR OPEN WATER.

THE SUBMARINE GETS STUCK ON A CORAL REEF AS IT TRIES TO ESCAPE.

THE SUB MANAGES TO FREE ITSELF AND SUBMERGE. *HELM* FAILS TO HIT IT. THE JAPANESE VESSEL VANISHES UNDERWATER.

JUST BEYOND THE HARBOR ENTRANCE, *HELM* SPOTS A SMALL SUBMARINE ON THE SURFACE AND OPENS FIRE.

8:25 A.M. MEANWHILE, CIVILIANS ARE RESPONDING TO THE ATTACK. FIRE ENGINES RACE TO HICKAM FIELD TO HELP, BUT THEY ARE ATTACKED BY ZEROES. FOUR FIREMEN ARE KILLED.

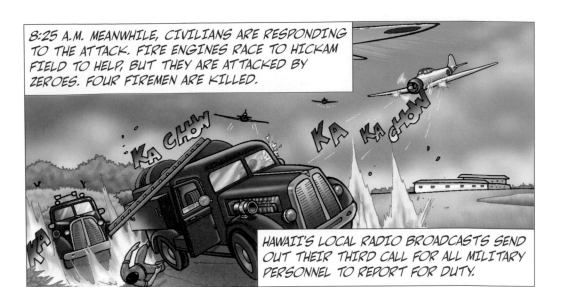

HAWAII'S LOCAL RADIO BROADCASTS SEND OUT THEIR THIRD CALL FOR ALL MILITARY PERSONNEL TO REPORT FOR DUTY.

ADMIRAL KIMMEL WATCHES HIS FLEET BEING BLOWN TO BITS.

HOW COULD THEY?

A SPENT BULLET SMASHES THROUGH HIS WINDOW AND HITS KIMMEL IN THE CHEST. IT KNOCKS HIM BACK A FEW STEPS, SURPRISING HIM.

IT WOULD HAVE BEEN MERCIFUL HAD IT KILLED ME.

AT FORD ISLAND, THE DESTROYER U.S.S. *MONAGHAN* HEADS TOWARD MIDDLE LOCH. IT PICKS ITS WAY THROUGH THE SHIPS AND SMOKE THAT NOW CLOG THE HARBOR.

8:39 A.M. AT MIDDLE LOCH, THE MOORED SEAPLANE TENDER U.S.S. *CURTIS* FIRES ON A SUB ON THE SURFACE.

A SHELL BLASTS THE SUB'S CONNING TOWER, JUST AS IT FIRES TWO TORPEDOES.

THE TORPEDOES GO WIDE. *MONAGHAN* SEES *CURTIS* FIRING ON THE SUB AND RAMS THE ENEMY VESSEL.

EVEN THOUGH IT RISKS DAMAGING ITS OWN STERN, *MONAGHAN* DROPS DEPTH CHARGES -- BUT THE SUB HAS VANISHED.

MONAGHAN SAILS AWAY, MAKING IT TO OPEN WATER -- JUST AS ANOTHER ATTACK BY THE JAPANESE BEGINS.

31

8:50 A.M. **NEVADA** ALSO STARTS TO SAIL OUT OF THE HARBOR. HER GUNS ARE FIRING FURIOUSLY.

ON BOARD, A SAILOR LOOKS AT THE STARS AND STRIPES OF THE AMERICAN FLAG. HE STARTS SINGING THE NATIONAL ANTHEM ...

OH, SAY, CAN YOU SEE...

9:00 A.M. 78 VALS FROM THE SECOND JAPANESE WAVE OF ATTACK BEGIN THEIR ASSAULT. THEY FIRE ON TARGETS MISSED BY THE FIRST ATTACK ON BATTLESHIP ROW, FORD ISLAND, AND THE NAVY YARD.

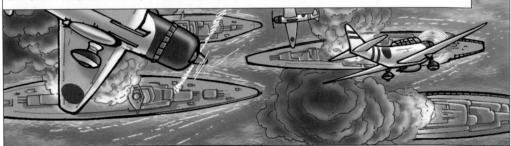

9:10 A.M. 23 VALS FROM **KAGA** FLY TOWARD **NEVADA**. THEY HOPE TO SINK IT AND CLOG UP THE HARBOR.

THE ATTACK IS FOCUSED, AND THE BATTLESHIP TAKES THREE HITS TO HER BOW.

ONE OF THE VALS IS SHOT DOWN BY ANTIAIRCRAFT FIRE.

FIRES RAGE ON THE FRONT OF THE SHIP.

THE FIRES BURN FOR 48 HOURS.

9:15 A.M. TWO MORE BOMBS STRIKE THE FORECASTLE AND TRIPOD MASTS. SEVERAL CREWMEN ARE KILLED.

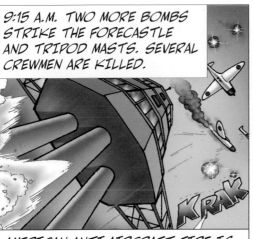

AMERICAN ANTI-AIRCRAFT FIRE IS VERY HEAVY BY NOW. ONE VAL IS HIT 22 TIMES.

NEVADA IS STARTING TO SINK LOW INTO THE WATER.

9:20 A.M. RATHER THAN RISK BLOCKING THE HARBOR, THE SHIP'S COMMANDER DECIDES TO GROUND HER IN SHALLOW WATER.

MEANWHILE, OTHER U.S. AIRCRAFT ARE STRUGGLING TO GET INTO THE AIR.

AT HALEIWA FIELD, JOHN DAINS IS ONE OF FOUR PILOTS WHO GET AIRBORNE IN P-36S AND P-40S.

MINUTES BEFORE, AT 8:55 A.M., 18 KATE HIGH-ALTITUDE BOMBERS ARRIVE OVER KANEOHE NAVAL AIR STATION.

THEIR BOMBS DESTROY HANGARS AND START HUGE FIRES.

THEY ARRIVE AT THE FIELD JUST AS SECOND LIEUTENANT WHITEMAN AND LIEUTENANT BISHOP ARE TAKING OFF IN THEIR P-40S.

WHITEMAN IS KILLED WHEN HIS AIRCRAFT IS SHOT DOWN AND CRASHES ON THE RUNWAY.

BISHOP MAKES IT OFF THE RUNWAY BUT HE CANNOT GAIN ALTITUDE. HE IS AN EASY TARGET FOR THE JAPANESE AIRCRAFT.

HE SURVIVES A CRASH INTO THE SEA AND WADES ASHORE. HE IS UNHURT.

SIX ZEROES FIRE AT THE B-17 THAT CRASHED AT BELLOWS EARLIER.

THEY ARE WASTING AMMUNITION. THE BOMBER IS ALREADY A WRECK.

AT KANEOHE NAVAL AIR STATION, CHIEF ORDNANCEMAN JOHN WILLIAM FINN GRABS A 50-CALIBER MACHINE GUN AND STARTS FIRING.

FINN IS WOUNDED SEVERAL TIMES BUT HITS A NUMBER OF JAPANESE AIRCRAFT. HIS HEROISM LATER WINS HIM THE MEDAL OF HONOR.

BY THE END OF THE JAPANESE ATTACK, 33 OF KANEOHE'S 37 PBY PLANES HAVE BEEN DESTROYED ...

... BUT THE JAPANESE DON'T HAVE IT ALL THEIR OWN WAY.

FOUR P-36S FROM WHEELER FIELD HAVE GOTTEN OFF THE GROUND AND FLY TO KANEOHE.

IN THE FOLLOWING AIR BATTLE, GORDON STERLING AND HIS P-36 ARE SHOT DOWN. STERLING AND HIS PLANE ARE NEVER FOUND.

THE P-36S DOWN TWO ZEROES AND LEAVE ANOTHER BARELY ABLE TO MAKE IT BACK TO ITS CARRIER.

MEANWHILE, AT 9:05 A.M., VALS ARRIVING OVER PEARL HARBOR FIND THAT THE EASY WELCOME EXPERIENCED BY THE FIRST WAVE OF ATTACKS HAS PASSED.

THE VALS CONTINUE TO FLY IN ON THEIR TARGETS.

HEAVY AMERICAN ANTIAIRCRAFT FIRE GREETS THEM.

BOMBS STRIKE THE DESTROYERS *CASSIN* AND *DOWNES* IN DRY DOCK. AMMUNITION ON BOARD *CASSIN* VIOLENTLY EXPLODES.

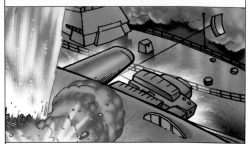

CASSIN ROLLS OVER AND SMASHES INTO THE *DOWNES*.

TWO VALS MAKE A FIRING PASS AT THE U.S.S. *BLUE* AS THE CRUISER TRIES TO GET OUT OF THE HARBOR.

THE CRUISER THEN ATTACKS A SUBMARINE IT THINKS IS BELOW WITH DEPTH CHARGES.

ONE IS HIT BY *BLUE'S* GUNFIRE AND IT CRASHES INTO THE SEA.

BUBBLES AND OIL ON THE SURFACE OF THE WATER SEEM TO INDICATE IT HAS HIT ITS TARGET.

9:20 A.M. THE JAPANESE KEEP HITTING HARD. THE U.S. PACIFIC NAVAL FLEET IS COLLAPSING UNDER THE ATTACK.

PENNSYLVANIA AND HONOLULU SINKING IN DRY DOCK ... RALEIGH, HIT AGAIN AND BARELY UPRIGHT ...

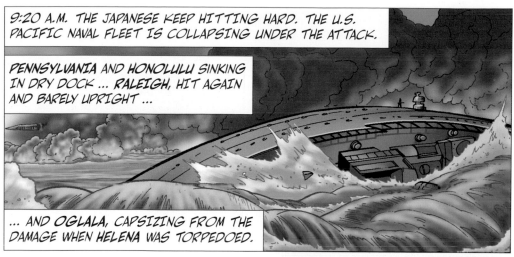

... AND OGLALA, CAPSIZING FROM THE DAMAGE WHEN HELENA WAS TORPEDOED.

9:30 A.M. THE FLOATING DRY DOCK THAT HOLDS THE DESTROYER SHAW IS HIT BY FIVE BOMBS, AND SINKS AROUND IT.

THEN THE SHAW'S FRONT AMMUNITION STORE EXPLODES. THE BLAST BLOWS OFF THE ENTIRE FRONT OF THE SHIP.

9:40 A.M. THE CRUISER ST. LOUIS HAS ESCAPED THE ATTACK WITHOUT DAMAGE.

HOWEVER, A CABLE BLOCKS ITS WAY OUT OF THE HAR-BOR.

ST. LOUIS TEARS THROUGH THE CABLE AND RACES FOR THE SEA.

10:04 A.M. ST. LOUIS CLEARS THE HARBOR BUT SUDDENLY SPOTS A PAIR OF TORPEDOES COMING TOWARD IT.

THE TORPEDOES MISS AND SLAM INTO A NEARBY CORAL REEF.

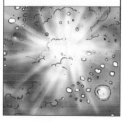

ST. LOUIS IS THE LAST VESSEL TO ESCAPE PEARL HARBOR DURING THE ATTACK.

9:50 A.M. SCHOFIELD BARRACKS, NOT FAR FROM WHEELER FIELD. THE BARRACKS WAS FIRED AT SEVERAL TIMES DURING THE COURSE OF THE ATTACK.

LIEUTENANT STEPHEN SALTZMAN AND SERGEANT LOWELL KLATT HEAR AN AIRCRAFT ENGINE. THEY GRAB BROWNING AUTOMATIC RIFLES AND RUN OUTSIDE.

THEY FIRE THEIR WEAPONS INTO THE FIGHTER THAT IS FLYING OVERHEAD.

THEY DO NOT STOP TO SEE WHAT TYPE OF PLANE IT IS.

THE AIRCRAFT TRAILS SMOKE AND DROPS OUT OF SIGHT.

THE BODY OF U.S. PILOT JOHN DAINS WAS LATER FOUND WITH IT.

10:00 A.M. JAPANESE AIRCRAFT FROM THE FIRST ATTACK RETURN TO THE CARRIERS WAITING FOR THEM.

THE ATTACK ISN'T OVER. EWA, WHEELER, AND HICKAM ARE BOMBARDED AGAIN.

AT HICKAM, THE B-17S ARE BLASTED TO BITS. AFTER THREE REPEATED ATTACKS, THE LAST ZEROES LEAVE.

A LONE ZERO FLIES A DAMAGE ASSESSMENT MISSION AT 900 FEET. THE PILOT'S REPORT IS SHORT AND TO THE POINT ...

INFLICTED MUCH DAMAGE.

11:00 A.M. COMMANDER FUCHIDA ALSO CIRCLES PEARL HARBOR TO REVIEW THE DAMAGE.

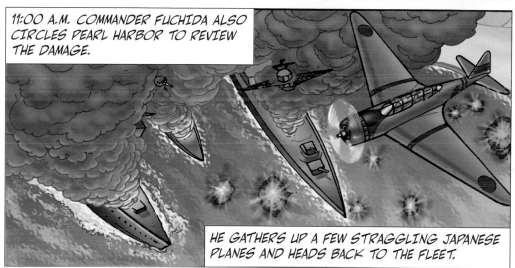

HE GATHERS UP A FEW STRAGGLING JAPANESE PLANES AND HEADS BACK TO THE FLEET.

HOWEVER, NOT EVERYONE IS GOING BACK WITH HIM. 29 PLANES HAVE BEEN SHOT DOWN. ONE SUBMARINE AND FIVE MIDGET SUBMARINES HAVE BEEN SUNK. 185 JAPANESE ARE DEAD.

NOON. AS MANY WORKING U.S. AIRCRAFT AS POSSIBLE SET OUT TO LOOK FOR THE JAPANESE FLEET. THEY FIND NOTHING.

THE JAPANESE LOSSES ARE TINY COMPARED TO THOSE THEY HAVE CAUSED...

... AND NOT JUST AMONG SAILORS, SOLDIERS, AND AIRMEN.

GIVE MORPHINE TO ANYONE IN PAIN AND MARK THEM!

THERE ARE MANY CIVILIAN CASUALTIES. THE HOSPITALS ARE OVERWHELMED WITH THE INJURED.

EVERY SCHOOL, BARRACKS, AND MESS HALL BECOMES A FIELD HOSPITAL TO HELP THE LARGE NUMBER OF WOUNDED.

MANY ARE GIVEN A SHOT OF THE VERY STRONG PAINKILLER, MORPHINE.

NURSES MARK PATIENTS' FOREHEADS WITH LIPSTICK TO MAKE SURE THEY AREN'T GIVEN A SECOND DEADLY DOSE.

1:00 P.M. JAPANESE COMMANDER FUCHIDA LANDS BACK ABOARD THE CARRIER *AKAGI* AND DELIVERS HIS REPORT.

AFTER DISCUSSING THE ATTACK WITH FUCHIDA, VICE-ADMIRAL NAGUMO DECIDES AGAINST A THIRD STRIKE AT THE AMERICANS.

HE FEARS A FURIOUS AMERICAN DEFENSE. ALSO, THE JAPANESE FLEET'S FUEL SUPPLY IS LOW AND A THIRD STRIKE WOULD TAKE THEM INTO NIGHT OPERATIONS -- SOMETHING HIS PILOTS ARE NOT USED TO.

NAGUMO ALSO FEARS A COUNTER-STRIKE FROM THE U.S. CARRIERS ...

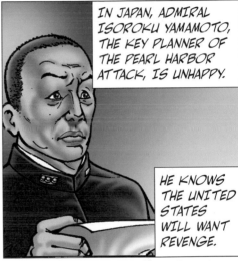

...EVEN THOUGH THE REST OF THE U.S. FLEET HAS ALMOST BEEN DESTROYED.

IN JAPAN, ADMIRAL ISOROKU YAMAMOTO, THE KEY PLANNER OF THE PEARL HARBOR ATTACK, IS UNHAPPY.

HE KNOWS THE UNITED STATES WILL WANT REVENGE.

ON HAWAII, THERE ARE FALSE REPORTS AND RUMORS OF INVADING JAPANESE SOLDIERS AND MORE AIR ATTACKS.

U.S. TROOPS PREPARE FOR AN INVASION. MARTIAL LAW IS DECLARED.

THE INVASION NEVER COMES. BUT ON THE NIGHT OF DECEMBER 7, A BLACKOUT ORDER IS ENFORCED.

IT IS OBSERVED FOR YEARS TO COME.

AMERICAN LOSSES ARE HIGH: 2,388 ARE KILLED, INCLUDING 48 CIVILIANS. 1,109 ARE WOUNDED (35 ARE CIVILIANS).

EIGHT BATTLESHIPS ARE SUNK OR NEARLY DESTROYED AND 11 OTHER VESSELS ARE SUNK AND BADLY DAMAGED. 169 AIRCRAFT ARE RIPPED APART.

HOWEVER, ONLY THREE VESSELS, *OKLAHOMA*, *ARIZONA*, AND *UTAH*, WOULD NOT BE REPAIRED AND RETURNED TO BATTLE.

ON DECEMBER 8, ONLY HOURS AFTER THE ATTACK ON HAWAII, JAPANESE FORCES INVADE THE MALAYA PENINSULA, HONG KONG, THE PHILIPPINES, THAILAND, AND WAKE ISLAND.

ON DECEMBER 10, JAPANESE AIRCRAFT SINK THE BRITISH BATTLESHIPS HMS *PRINCE OF WALES* AND *REPULSE* IN THE SOUTH CHINA SEA.

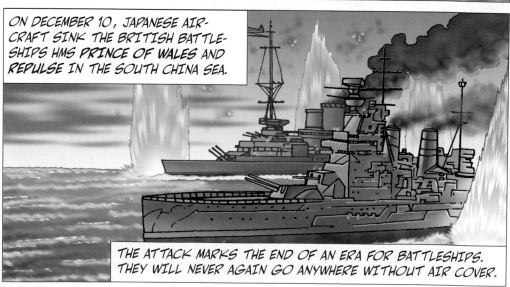

THE ATTACK MARKS THE END OF AN ERA FOR BATTLESHIPS. THEY WILL NEVER AGAIN GO ANYWHERE WITHOUT AIR COVER.

12:20 P.M., DECEMBER 8. U.S. PRESIDENT FRANKLIN D. ROOSEVELT ADDRESSES CONGRESS.

YESTERDAY, DECEMBER 7, 1941 -- A DATE THAT WILL LIVE IN INFAMY -- THE UNITED STATES OF AMERICA WAS SUDDENLY AND DELIBERATELY ATTACKED BY THE NAVAL AND AIR FORCES OF THE EMPIRE OF JAPAN.

HE ASKS FOR AND IS GIVEN THE AUTHORITY TO DECLARE WAR ON JAPAN. HE SIGNS THE DECLARATION OF WAR THAT DAY.

OVER THE NEXT FEW MONTHS, THE AMERICAN SHIPS ARE REFLOATED, REPAIRED, AND THROWN INTO BATTLE AGAINST THE JAPANESE.

FIRST TO BE READY IS NEVADA, ON APRIL 19, 1942.

JUNE 1945. THE BATTLESHIPS THAT BARELY ESCAPED DESTRUCTION AT PEARL HARBOR ARE ON HAND TO SEE OKINAWA FALL -- THE LAST STEPPING-STONE TO JAPAN ITSELF.

LESS THAN A MONTH LATER, THE WAR IS OVER. JAPAN LIES IN RUINS.

THE END

AFTERMATH

Admiral Yamamoto's concerns about the poorly timed breaking off of peace talks with the United States were correct. The official Japanese declaration of war was not received until the day after the attack. By then, America was enraged by what looked like a surprise attack. However, even if the message sent by the Japanese government had arrived at its 1:00 P.M. deadline, America would have reacted in a similar fashion. The United States jumped into action. Its people united against the enemy, and American industry geared up for war.

On December 11, Nazi Germany, under Adolph Hitler, declared war on America. Germany had signed an agreement with Japan and Italy, supporting these countries in the event of war. Hitler's actions further enraged the American public. Before the attack on Pearl Harbor, many

The attack on Pearl Harbor caused huge damage. Many people died and all of the U.S. fleet's battleships were sunk or nearly destroyed.

Americans opposed entering the war in Europe. They wanted America to remain neutral, refusing to choose sides between Britain and her allies and Nazi Germany.

The attack also dealt a terrible blow to the U.S. Navy's Pacific Fleet. The remaining ships in the fleet could do nothing to stop the expansion of the Japanese empire into much of Southeast Asia and the southwest Pacific.

However, the U.S. Navy was far from defeated. American muscle soon had the damaged ships back in action. Those ships destroyed beyond saving were stripped of all useful parts.

The U.S. Navy could also consider itself fortunate that its valuable aircraft carriers were spared. *Lexington* and *Enterprise* were at sea during the attack, while *Saratoga* was in San Diego. This would prove vital in the coming months when the carriers and their aircraft would help inflict the first defeats on the Japanese at the battles of the Coral Sea and Midway. While the loss of the battleships was important to the Americans, it soon became clear that they were not as vital to winning the war at sea as Japan believed.

Admiral Yamamoto's fear of a long war with America also proved correct. In June 1942, Japan suffered a crushing defeat at the Battle of Midway from which it never recovered. The war in the Pacific would rage on for three more years, finally ending with the dropping of two atomic bombs on Japan in August 1945.

The attack on Pearl Harbor had, indeed, awakened the American sleeping giant. The course of history was forever changed because of the events on that bright Sunday morning in December 1941.

After the success of Pearl Harbor, the Japanese went on to launch other air attacks on the Americans, including those at the battles of Midway and the Coral Sea.

45

antiaircraft Designed for defense against air attack.

assessment The act of determining the importance, size, or value of something.

auxiliary Additional, subsidiary, or supplementary.

battleship A class of warship of the largest size, having the heaviest guns and armor.

berth A space at a wharf for a ship to dock or anchor; to bring a ship to a berth.

buoyancy The capacity to float in a liquid.

capsize To overturn or cause to overturn.

civilian A person not serving in the armed forces.

cruiser A medium-sized warship of high speed and a large cruising range, with less armor and firepower than a battleship.

depth charge An explosive charge designed for use underwater.

destroyer A small, fast, highly maneuverable warship armed with missiles, guns, torpedoes, and depth charges.

forecastle mast The upright pole that supports the sails and rigging of a ship, which here is located in the forecastle, the front section of a ship's upper deck.

infamy An extreme and publicly known criminal or evil act.

list To tilt to one side.

martial law Military rule of a civilian population imposed for a time, as in an emergency or during a war.

minesweeper A warship designed for removing mines by dragging.

moor To fix in place; to make fast by means of lines or anchors.

prelude An introductory action or event preceding a more important matter.

radar The equipment used to detect distant objects and determine their characteristics by causing radio waves to be reflected from them and analyzing the results.

resolute Firm or determined; unwavering.

sabotage The deliberate damage or destruction of property, or an act that interferes with work or another activity.

starboard The right-hand side of a ship as one faces forward.

strafe To attack with machine-gun fire from low-flying aircraft.

straggling Falling behind.

submerge To place under water.

ORGANIZATIONS

National Museum of the Pacific War
340 East Main Street
Fredericksburg, TX 78624
(830) 997-4379
Web site: http://www.nimitz-museum.com/index.htm

National Park Service
USS Arizona Memorial
1 Arizona Memorial Place
Honolulu, HI 96818
(808) 422-0561
Web site: www.nps.gov/usar/

FOR FURTHER READING

Allen, Thomas B. *Remember Pearl Harbor*. Washington, DC: National Geographic Children's Books, 2001.

Krensky, Stephen. *Pearl Harbor*. London: Aladdin Children's Books, 2001.

Mazel, Harry. *A Boy at War: A Novel of Pearl Harbor*. London: Aladdin Children's Books, 2002.

Salisbury, Graham. *Under the Blood-Red Sun*. New York: Yearling Books, 1995.

Smith, Carl. *Pearl Harbor 1941: The Day of Infamy*. Oxford, England: Osprey Publishing, 2001.

WEB SITES

Due to the changing nature of Internet links, the Rosen Publishing Group, Inc., has developed an online list of Web sites related to the subject of this book. This site is updated regularly. Please use this link to access the list:

http://www.rosenlinks.com/gbww2/ph